The Great Court a... ...um
Kenneth Powell

SPACES

The British Museum's Great Court – the Queen Elizabeth II Great Court as it is formally known – is one of the most spectacular interiors of any of the world's great museums, a major work by Britain's most eminent living architect, Norman Foster, and the largest enclosed public space in Europe. Though made possible only by the application of state-of-the-art computer design techniques and the use of modern materials, the Great Court is arguably a realisation of the Enlightenment ideals that inspired the foundation of the British Museum more than 250 years ago. It has transformed the Museum both as a visitor experience and, with its associated new galleries and education facilities, extended the resources of the Museum as a place where its collections can be more fully displayed, enjoyed and understood. But above all, it is a majestic work of architecture and engineering, part of a great British tradition but equally a landmark in the emergence of London as a global centre of culture and learning for the 21st century.

The British Museum celebrated its 250th birthday in 2003. The Museum was established by Act of Parliament in June 1753. Its core collection was that amassed by Sir Hans Sloane, Bt. (1660–1753),

◀ An engraving of Montagu House, circa 1830. Situated in London's Bloomsbury district, it housed the original British Museum, which opened in 1759.

physician and antiquary, containing "plants, fossils, minerals, zoological, anatomical and pathological specimens, antiquities and artificial curiosities, prints, drawings and coins, books and manuscripts." The funds for the acquisition of the collection, which, by the terms of Sloane's will, was to be offered first to the nation, were raised by means of a lottery. (Nearly a century and a half later, the newly established National Lottery was to be a generous backer of the Great Court project.) Lottery money also allowed the new institution to acquire the great libraries founded by Sir Robert Cotton (1570–1631) and Robert Harley, 1st Earl of Oxford (1661–1724) which included outstandingly important Anglo-Saxon and medieval manuscripts – the Lindisfarne Gospels, for example. There were ideas of constructing a new building to house all these treasures but, for the time being, British pragmatism prevailed and an existing building, Montagu House in Bloomsbury, on the site of the present Museum building and standing in seven acres of grounds, was purchased for £10,000 and adapted. The British Museum opened to the public in 1759, but initially public access was extremely limited – there was a waiting list for tickets, issued by written application

only, and very limited opening hours. Not until 1810 was relatively free access allowed to "any person of decent appearance" and even then the building was open for only three days a week. Well into the Victorian period the presence of armed sentries at the Museum gates gave the impression that the building was as much of a fortress as the Bank of England.

The British Museum's collections grew steadily over the half century or so following its opening, as the new era of exploration and colonisation dawned. The acquisition of the famous Elgin Marbles in 1816 was a landmark in the Museum's development. Even more significant was the purchase in 1823 (for £180,000, discreetly paid, it is alleged, to King George IV) of the magnificent library assembled by the king's father, George III. This acquisition provided the final catalyst for development plans that had been under consideration for some years, the aim being to replace Montagu House with a purpose-built museum building. Sir Robert Smirke (1780–1867) was appointed architect for the project, proposing a huge structure in the Greek Revival style (of which he was a prime exponent) arranged around a central quadrangle. Not until 1847, when the last remnant of Montagu House was torn

◀ The King's Library, in the East Wing (1827) that was specially built to house it. The photograph dates from 1875. Since 2003, this exquisite room has hosted the gallery of the Enlightenment.

down, was Smirke's scheme effectively completed – though there were further additions over the next 50 years, culminating in the King Edward VII galleries, opened in 1914, which terminate the Museum to the north.

Despite the huge scale of its premises, the British Museum survived only by gradually hiving off parts of its immense collection. Paintings were transferred to the new National Gallery in 1825. The natural history specimens went to a spectacular new building (the Natural History Museum, designed by Alfred Waterhouse) in South Kensington in the 1880s. The ethnographical collections, most of which had been in store for many years, were housed in Burlington Gardens, off Piccadilly, for nearly 30 years in what was known as the Museum of Mankind. (The departure of the British Library from the British Museum would allow the collection to return to Bloomsbury.)

The first part of Robert Smirke's Museum to be completed (in 1827) was the wing along the eastern side of the site containing the King's Library with its 65,000 precious volumes. At 300 feet (91.44 metres) long and richly decorated in refined Neoclassical style, it remains the finest of Smirke's interiors. (It was

◀ The famous round Reading
Room, designed by Sydney
Smirke, under construction.
This 1855 photograph
shows the iron framework
almost completed.

restored in 2003 to pristine condition as the Museum's
gallery of the Enlightenment.) This space, often
described as one of the finest rooms in London, both
complements and forms a striking contrast to the
adjacent Great Court.

Books and manuscripts formed a fundamental
element in the British Museum's collections from the
beginning. Only in 1972 were they formally divorced
from the Museum with the establishment of the British
Library, initially co-existing with the Museum on
the Bloomsbury site. By 1848 the British Museum
possessed 435,000 books and was acquiring more at

the rate of 30,000 a year. (Copyright acts stipulated that it should receive a copy of every book published in Britain.) There were seats for only 200 readers, usually oversubscribed. The round Reading Room, restored as part of the Great Court project after being vacated by the British Library, represented the Museum's response to the steady growth of book stocks and readers.

The round Reading Room was the idea of Italian-born Sir Anthony Panizzi (1797–1879), a political refugee who was Keeper of Printed Books from 1837 and Principal Librarian from 1856. There were a number of precedents for circular library buildings, not least James Gibbs' Radcliffe Camera, part of the Bodleian Library in Oxford. The Frenchman Benjamin Delessert had made designs for a circular Royal Library in Paris (1835) which may have influenced the London project. The first proposal for a circular structure (housing sculpture) in Smirke's central quadrangle was made by Prof William Hosking of King's College, London, in 1848 but it was to Robert Smirke's brother Sydney that Panizzi turned to develop his own vision of the new library.

There was little opposition to the idea of building in the quadrangle: Charles Barry, architect of the new Houses of Parliament, proposed roofing it over with an iron and glass canopy to provide a "Hall of Antiquities" – a premonition of the Great Court concept. Envisaged originally as a pleasant green oasis at the heart of the Museum building, the quadrangle was in reality closed to visitors and described as "a dull, miserable space" and, with some degree of exaggeration perhaps, as "a mere well of malaria, a pestilent congregation of vapours". (It was home to a large number of feral cats.) The buildings surrounding the quadrangle had been completed, in fact, only a few years previously when Panizzi and Smirke's scheme to fill in the space emerged in 1852. The Reading Room, completed in 1857 at a cost of £150,000, was a structure of brick, concrete and iron – 2,000 tons of it forming the ribs supporting the dome – which are infilled on the inside with a patent papier mâché. Measuring 140 feet in diameter (just two feet less than the mighty Pantheon in Rome), the Reading Room was loved by some critics, loathed by others, but quickly became one of the most

◄ A reader in the Reading Room, 1952, fills in a form to ask for a book that is kept in the stacks.

▶ Vladimir Ilich Ulyanov used the Reading Room between 1902 and 1911 under a number of guises: employing either his real name, or pseudonyms including Jacob Richter (as in this 1902 form, claiming his reader's ticket), or (as he is best known) Lenin.

famous spaces in London. It was virtually a home from home for British writers such as Hardy, Dickens, Kipling and Shaw, and for exiles who famously included Marx and Lenin.

Conceived as a free-standing drum in the quadrangle, the Reading Room had space for over a million books but the shelving provided soon proved inadequate in the face of the growing tide of acquisitions. The existence of the central quadrangle was virtually forgotten as every part of it was progressively filled with bookstacks occupying the four quadrants of the space. (The south portico, intended as the point of entry to the courtyard, was removed in 1870 to make way for the extension of the Museum's entrance hall.) For most visitors, the Reading Room, beloved of its users, was forbidden territory, open only to those with readers' tickets, an apparent void at the centre of the Museum. Negotiating a way through the building from south to north meant a long trudge through the perimeter galleries and via a number of stairs, so these galleries tended to be crowded not only with visitors looking at the exhibits but also with those simply passing through.

By the post-war years the library was regarded increasingly as a cuckoo in the nest, inexorably expand-ing into space that simply did not exist. For readers, the removal of many books to stores away from Blooms-bury – newspapers moved out to north London as early as 1905 – proved a constant irritation. So the idea was born of a new library. In 1962 Leslie Martin and Colin St John Wilson were appointed to design it. The site, identified a decade earlier, was the area immediately south of the Museum beyond Great Russell Street. Martin and St John Wilson proposed demolishing every building there apart from Hawksmoor's baroque church of St George, Bloomsbury and creating not only a library with seats for 1,100 readers but also shops,

offices and housing for some of the 900 people displaced by the scheme.

The proposals were controversial from the beginning. The threatened area was one of immense character and charm, full of bookshops, galleries, pubs and cafes, which still provide an appropriate backdrop to the formal splendours of the Museum. By 1971, the scheme, though slightly reduced in scale, had risen in price to £36 million while the conservationist case against it grew ever more vociferous. By 1974 the case for demolishing a whole quarter of London was lost. St John Wilson, who had carried the project forward

▶ The Reading Room, circa 1925.

after Martin's retirement, was commissioned by the British Library Board in 1975 to develop plans for an alternative site next to St Pancras station, half a mile north of the Museum. After many vicissitudes, construction of the new British Library began in 1984 and the new building was completed in 1997, though it was to be December 1998 before the last of the books left Bloomsbury.

With the new British Library under construction, the British Museum was able to consider the future of the spaces that the library had occupied for so long. There was a conviction that the time had come for radical thinking about the future of the Museum, faced with

◀ The interior of the cupola at the New German Parliament, Reichstag building, Berlin, designed by Foster and Partners (1992–99).

nearly six million visitors annually and visitor facilities that compared poorly with those of other great world museums. Paris's Grand Louvre project in particular, one of the *grands projets* launched by President François Mitterrand, demonstrated the potential for injecting new life into a historic institution. Could London achieve something on this scale?

As early as 1989, a target date of 2003, the Museum's 250th birthday, was set for the completion of the redevelopment. Retention of the Reading Room as a library of some sort was regarded as vital. It was assumed that the surrounding book stacks would be

▶ The Carré d'Art, Nîmes, designed by Foster and Partners (1984–92). Like the Reichstag and the Great Court, this project was a happy marriage of a great historic building with contemporary architecture.

demolished to make space for offices, storage spaces, educational facilities and a much-needed lecture theatre. The shops and cafes that museum visitors now regard as a basic necessity were to be accommodated. The return of the ethnographical collections from Burlington Gardens was another high priority. There was, in short, a great deal that had to be found a place within the space potentially available. With Dr Robert Anderson, formerly director of the Museum of Scotland, as Director, the Museum launched an architectural competition in 1993. It received 132 expressions of interests from architectural practices

worldwide, of which 22 were shortlisted and asked to develop their ideas. Finally, a shortlist of three practices, Arup Associates, Foster and Partners, and Rick Mather Associates, was announced. Foster and Partners was formally named as winner in July 1994.

The practice, founded by Norman Foster as Foster Associates in 1967, was internationally renowned for buildings such as the Sainsbury Centre, Norwich, the Hongkong & Shanghai Bank headquarters in Hong Kong and the terminal building at Stansted Airport. In 1992 it had been appointed to rebuild the Reichstag building in Berlin as the new seat of the German

▶ Architectural plans submitted for
planning approval in December 1995:
auditorium level, courtyard level,
Hotung Gallery level, restaurant level.

Parliament. Works such as the Carré d'Art in the French
city of Nîmes and the Sackler Galleries at London's
Royal Academy of Arts demonstrated Foster's ability
to work in an entirely modern way within an historic
context. Within the practice, one of Norman Foster's
long standing partners, Spencer de Grey, who had led
the Sackler Galleries project, assumed responsibility
for the Great Court project, seeing it through to
completion. Giles Robinson was appointed as Foster's
project architect.

In fact, Foster and Partners' competition-winning
British Museum scheme differed in a number of significant respects from that eventually built. The quadrangle around the Reading Room was to be covered, but
with a roof of ETFE (ethylenetetrafluoroethylene)
air-filled "pillows" rather than glass, supported on a
simple steel grid 14 feet (4.3 metres) square. The
advantage of using ETFE was that it was cheap and
very lightweight (and also offered good insulation),
but a fairly heavy structure was required to anchor the
pillows against wind. The Reading Room would be
girdled by an elliptical structure containing education

spaces, a lecture theatre, shops and a restaurant to
the north and south of Sydney Smirke's great drum, all
accessed by a ramp around the edge of the ellipse.
Bridges would connect this structure to the surrounding galleries on three sides. New exhibition galleries,
including one for ethnography, stores and staff
facilities would be located at two basement levels.

Although these proposals were subsequently to
be rethought quite radically, some fundamental
principles of the Great Court scheme were already
established, notably the provision of a pedestrian
route through the central space from south to north.
This would involve the removal of the North Library –
an extension of the Reading Room originally designed
by J. J. Burnet but somewhat spoiled by inter-war
alterations, which was functionally redundant anyway
– and the reinstatement of the demolished south
portico. Externally, the forecourt of the Museum, much
of which was used for parking, should be remodelled.
The significance of the Grade I listed British Museum
meant that these proposals had to be discussed with
bodies such as English Heritage, the government's

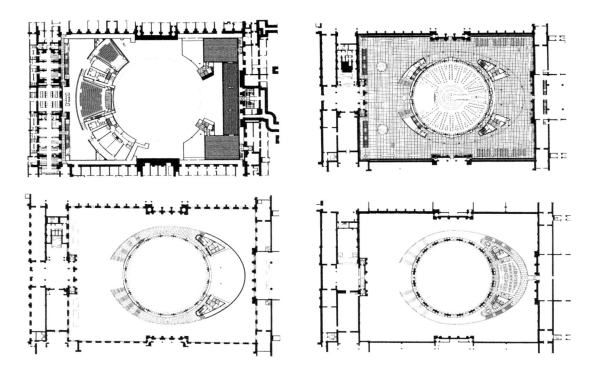

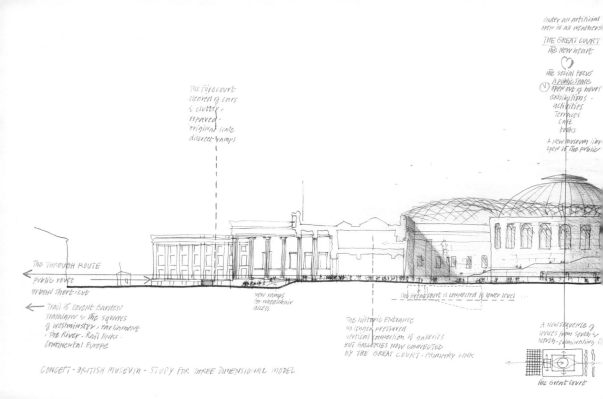

UNDER AN ARTIFICIAL
SKY IN ALL WEATHERS

THE GREAT COURT
THE NEW HEART

♡ the social focus
A PUBLIC SPACE
open one of hours
exhibitions ·
activities
Terraces
Café
books

A new museum line
open to the public

The Forecourt
cleared of cars
& clutter ·
repaved ·
original scale
discreet ramps

THE THROUGH ROUTE

public route

urban short-cut

← Trail to Covent Garden
Trafalgar & the squares
of Westminster · Parliament
· the River · Rail links ·
Continental Europe

New ramps
for disabled
access

The Great Court is connected to lower level ...

The historic entrance
no longer pressured
vertical connection to galleries
but galleries now connected
by THE GREAT COURT · PRIMARY LINK

A new sequence of
spaces from South to
North · culminating in
THE GREAT COURT

CONCEPT · BRITISH MUSEUM · STUDY FOR THREE DIMENSIONAL MODEL

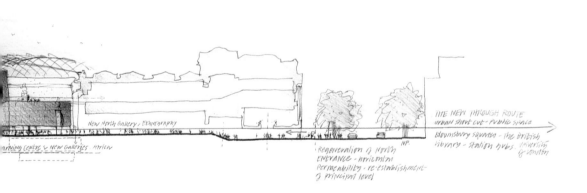

◄ Drawing by Norman Foster, illustrating how the Great Court would form the new heart of the museum as well as a new urban through route for London.

New North Gallery · Ethnography

rhing centre · New Galleries · Africa

Regeneration of North
ENTRANCE · horizontal
Permeability · re-establishment
of principal level

NP.

THE NEW THROUGH ROUTE
urban short cut · Public Space

Bloomsbury squares · the British
Library · station hubs · University
of London

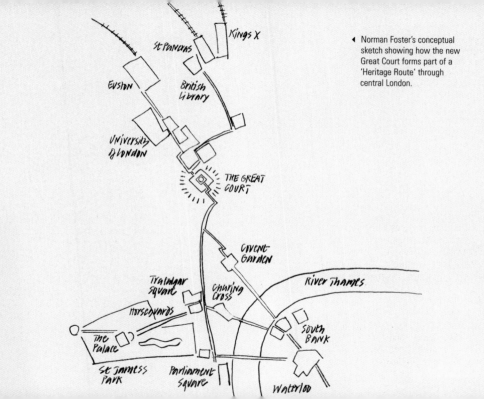

Kings X

St Pancras

Euston

British Library

University of London

THE GREAT COURT

Covent Garden

Trafalgar Square

Charing Cross

River Thames

Horseguards

The Palace

South Bank

St Jamess Park

Parliament Square

Waterloo

◄ Norman Foster's conceptual sketch showing how the new Great Court forms part of a 'Heritage Route' through central London.

▶ A plan of the museum at ground level, showing how the Great Court forms both a circulation hub and the focus of a new public route through the building.

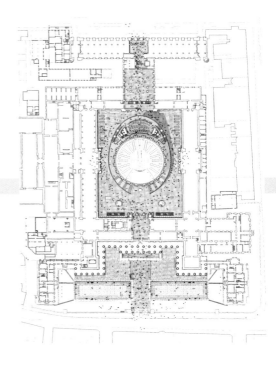

historic buildings watchdog, and the then Royal Fine Art Commission, as well as planners from the local authority, the London Borough of Camden.

During the year and a half following the appointment of Foster, the competition scheme was subjected to a searching process of analysis and evaluation involving the Museum's own team and the architects, as well as these outside bodies. It was felt that the elliptical structure, extending almost to the walls of the quadrangle to the north and south, filled too much of what was potentially a magnificent public space. A strategic study revealed that some of the facilities that

◀ Aerial view during demolition phase, 1998, showing the circular Reading Room inside the newly-revealed courtyard.

▶ An 1841 drawing by Robert Smirke of one of the south portico's four columns in Ionic style, which faced onto the courtyard. Demolished in 1877, the south portico was rebuilt in 1999 in the spirit of Smirke, with the help of this drawing.

had been included in the competition scheme, including offices and stores, could go elsewhere. By late 1995, the scheme had been substantially amended. The elliptical structure had been cut back so that it extended only to the north of the Reading Room, where it was connected to upper level galleries by a bridge; the other two bridges, seen as intrusions into the new court, were dropped from the scheme. It was to contain shops at ground level, with a temporary exhibition gallery (which became the Sir Joseph Hotung Gallery) above and a restaurant on top. Stepped ramps, rather than conventional stairs, were used to access the

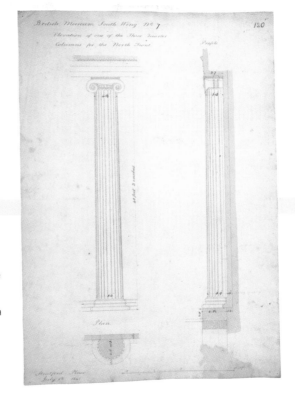

▸ Construction of the new roof
was carried out from a
platform 18 metres above
floor level.

upper levels. Basement development, always an expensive option, was to be limited to one level only.

The long-lost south portico was to be rebuilt as a structure in the spirit of Smirke rather than as an exact replica of what had been destroyed. As Spencer de Grey points out, the new portico was designed as "a reinvention of Smirke's original design. It stands further forward in the courtyard in order to accommodate two new lifts that provide access to all the Museum's public levels. We also added an attic window in the central bay to afford spectacular views into the Great Court from the Central Saloon, which is located on the upper level immediately behind the south portico. Interestingly, the provenance for such an opening was to be found in one of Smirke's original sketches." Ideas of opening up the portico by constructing just the columns and leaving open the intervening spaces were dropped after English Heritage opposed this approach.

The other major issue that was reconsidered was the nature of the roof structure that would form such a defining feature of the new Great Court. The heaviness of the steel grid required to anchor the ETFE pillows was seen as at odds with the desire to create a lightweight canopy for the space. Nor, on further

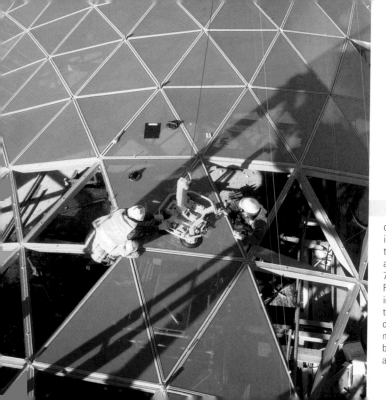

consideration, did the use of this material seem entirely
in tune with the dignity of the setting. It was decided
that glass had to be used instead. The roof had to cover
an area measuring 325 feet by 227 feet (100 metres by
70 metres) with the largest span (from the Reading
Room drum to the furthest corner of the court) extending to 130 feet (40 metres). A further complication was
the fact that the Reading Room does not even stand
centrally in the courtyard, but is slightly closer to the
north façade. The nature of the space meant that a roof
based on a square structural grid would not work and
a triangulated structure would be required. It was

◀ View of the roof under construction, looking from the north. The pediment of the museum's front entrance portico can be seen above the drum of the Reading Room.

▶ Over 14 months in 1999 and 2000, the glass roof structure transformed the skyline of the museum.

developed by the Foster team in consultation with engineers from the Buro Happold practice using a state-of-the-art computer programme. Even so, the design process took many months. The roof designs continued to be developed in detail after the planning application for the Great Court was submitted at the end of 1995. Planning and listed building consent was granted in January 1997, so that the scheme was set to go ahead as soon as the British Library had vacated the site.

As the Great Court scheme was developed, it became apparent that around £100 million would be needed to realise it. The tradition of state funding that had made possible President Mitterrand's extravagant *grands projets* did not exist in Britain. A huge boost to the project was provided, however, by the establishment of the new National Lottery in 1994. The bodies established to distribute Lottery profits to "good causes" included the Heritage Lottery Fund and the Millennium Commission, the latter body having a limited period of operation and a specific brief to fund projects that would celebrate the millennium in the year 2000. In March 1996, the Millennium Commission announced a grant of £30 million to the Great Court

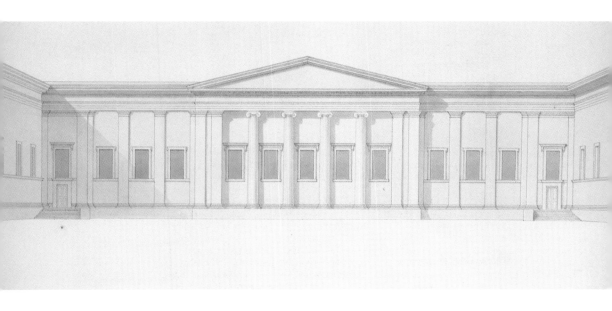

◀ Robert Smirke's 1833 drawing of the south elevation of the museum's North Wing. This façade, which faces into the courtyard, has now been restored to Smirke's original design.

project. A condition of the grant was that the Court should always be open to the public free of charge – there had been a brief attempt to impose an admission charge to the Museum during the 1970s – and that it should have extended opening hours beyond those of the Museum's galleries. Finally, and rather ominously, the Commission was insistent that the Great Court must be open to the public before the end of 2000. The construction team was adamant that work had to start on site early in 1998 if this demanding deadline was to be achieved. Significantly, the Great Court was opened on 6 December 2000, on time and on budget.

The remit of the Heritage Lottery Fund (HLF) was to fund specifically "heritage" projects. Its interest in the Great Court, therefore, was the restoration and conservation of the historic structures rather than new construction. In discussion with the HLF, the Museum and its architects developed proposals both to include elements of restoration in the Great Court scheme (for example, the reinstatement of the Smirke windows in the north façade of the courtyard) and to extend restoration work to other areas on the public route through the Museum. Back in the 1980s, when the front hall and staircase had been repainted, there had been

pressure from conservationists to restore the elaborate decorative scheme executed there in 1847 by the firm of Collman & Davis (probably to Sydney Smirke's designs but based on antique Greek and Roman precedents). The spaces had, however, been repainted in plain grey. Now the decision was taken that the 1847 scheme would be reinstated as part of the Great Court project. HLF money also paid for the replacement of the railings outside the King Edward VII Galleries, which had been taken for scrap during the Second World War. A grant of £15.75 million was subsequently agreed by the HLF. The Museum was still faced with the

challenge of raising more than half of the funding required for the project.

A development trust was established, with Sir Claus Moser as its chairman and HRH Princess Margaret as president, and the fundraising campaign was launched. Its success gave the Museum the confidence to proceed with the project. One donor, the Garfield Weston Foundation, gave £20 million. A series of individuals and foundations made generous contributions, along with the British Museum Friends and the American Friends of the British Museum, so that the requisite

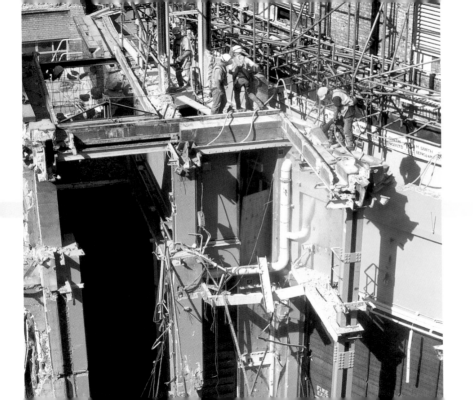

◀ The outside of the Reading Room's great drum, revealed during the process of demolition, 1998.
▶ Removal of the bookstacks revealed the damaged façades of the quadrangle. These were restored in the course of the Great Court project.

funding was in place a year before building work was completed.

With the British Library having vacated the Reading Room, the perimeter stacks and the North Library, work could start on site in spring 1998. Within six months, virtually all of the bookstacks that filled the courtyard had been demolished, a massive task in itself since more than 20,000 cubic metres of material had to be removed. (Only one of the original cast iron quadrant stacks, dating from the 1850s, survived, two having been rebuilt and a third destroyed by wartime bombing. This was carefully dismantled and put into store

after efforts to find a new home for it proved fruitless.)
Demolition material had to be lifted out of the courtyard
by a giant tower crane 150 feet (46 metres) high since it
could not be taken through the Museum building. The
results of the demolition process were both a revela-
tion – the scale of the courtyard and its potential to
become a public space were revealed – and a disap-
pointment. Damage to Smirke's courtyard facades was
worse than had been imagined, with columns ruthless-
ly lopped away by the builders of the book stacks.

The exterior of the Reading Room was revealed as
a very utilitarian brick structure, a striking contrast to

the elegant interior, with ugly rectangular window openings. Restoration and cleaning of the damaged courtyard facades, a lengthy process, involving specialist consultants and contractors, began almost immediately. The strategy adopted was to reinstate lost elements but not to attempt any replication of the elaborate detail of the Regency era. The restoration of the Reading Room, virtually a self-contained project, also began early in the construction programme.

The removal of the British Library raised a number of questions about the future of the Reading Room. Suggestions that the furnishings be removed and the space used as a spectacular gallery, perhaps for the display of large pieces of sculpture, were rejected. It was resolved that it should remain a library, but one open not just to scholars but to the general public. The not insubstantial libraries of the Museum's departments, mostly from the Department of Ethnography, could be housed there, filling the empty shelves in the upper galleries. Thanks to the generosity of the Paul Hamlyn Foundation, an open access library of around 25,000 volumes was subsequently provided on the ground floor shelves, while the COMPASS database, containing pictures and information on 4,000 items

▶ The exterior of the Reading Room, a utilitarian brick structure, but soon to be adorned with white limestone.

from the collections, can be accessed from terminals provided. Original furnishings were restored and retained. The Victorian ventilation system, with grilles set in the legs of the reading tables, was overhauled and supplemented by a new extract and smoke venting system installed around the edge of the rotunda.

The Reading Room had never received the decorative scheme that its architect planned. Proposals by the artist Alfred Stevens, best known for the monument to the Duke of Wellington in St Paul's Cathedral, remained unrealised and a relatively simple scheme executed instead. In 1907 the names of nineteen great British

◀ The museum's main entrance hall was, before restoration, typically all too crowded.

▶ The entrance hall after completion of the redevelopment, less busy now that the Great Court has become the focus of the museum; its original colour scheme was also restored.

◄ The interior of the Reading Room after renovation.

▶ Removing the scaffolding after restoration of the Reading Room, which now displays the original 1857 colour scheme of Sydney Smirke.

writers were inscribed in the panels over the cornice, but these were painted out in the 1950s. As part of the Great Court project Sydney Smirke's 1857 scheme, blue, cream and gold, was reinstated. The exterior of the Reading Room, as unadorned as the unfinished façade of an Italian cathedral, was clad in white lime-stone brought from quarries near Granada in Spain. A grand stone-clad staircase was wrapped around the drum to provide access to the spaces on the upper levels of the new structure to the north. The stone cladding, it was felt, helped to root the drum of the Reading Room to the floor of the court, also to be of

COURT CELEBRATING

stone (in this instance quarried in France), and to provide a solid contrast to the lightweight aesthetic of the roof. Spencer de Grey describes the completed Great Court as "a symphony of European limestones".

The idea of covering the central quadrangle of the Museum with glass was first promoted in the Victorian period: covered 'winter gardens' were a feature of 19th century hotels and public buildings. But the structural solution underpinning Foster's roof would have been inconceivable without modern steel and glazing technology and the use of computer design programmes. The roof was constructed in 14 months from a platform

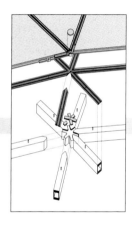

◀ Assembly diagram illustrating
how the specially-made steel
nodes and the glazed panels
fit together.
▶ The finished glazed roof,
viewed from below on the
floor of the Great Court.

58.5 feet (18 metres) above floor level. It is formed of 3,312 triangular panels, each one unique in shape – at one point, as many as 10,000 panels were envisaged. The steel components (more than 5,000 of them) were made in Vienna and shipped to Derby, where they were assembled into 152 prefabricated sections using specially made steel nodes and transported to London for craning into position. The glass panels were then inserted into the steel lattice, the last being installed on 13 July 2000 by the young daughter of architect Spencer de Grey. The roof contains 478 tonnes of steel and 315 tonnes of glass, yet there is no hint of heavi-

ness in its appearance. And though it peeps over the roofs of the galleries in some distant views, its form seems a natural evolution of the Victorian technology that generated the dome at its centre. By night, it forms a beacon of light when viewed from the air.

The great roof is perceived as the key element of the Great Court, but beneath it a complex of subsidiary spaces that are vital elements in the project was created. The floor level of the Great Court was raised to that of the front entrance hall. Sunk 29 feet (9 metres) below the floor level is the Clore Education Centre, with its two auditoria and five seminar rooms and approached

◀ The foyer of the Clore Education Centre, located in the basement beneath the courtyard.

▶ The larger of the two auditoria contained in the Clore Centre.

◀ ▶ Interior views of the
Sainsbury African
Galleries, located in
the basement level.

◀ Staircase leading from the courtyard to the basement level of the Great Court.

▶ Interior of the completed Great Court, with (in the foreground) a sculpture of a Roman horse and rider (1st–2nd centuries AD), one of the few works on display in the courtyard itself.

via staircases boldly cut into the floor of the court. Halfway down the stairs, ingeniously slotted into the brick vaults that support the Museum's main entrance, is the Ford Centre, providing facilities for the 1,500 school children who visit the Museum on a typical day. The Museum's education department now has more than 40 members of staff. Below the floor in the northern sector of the Great Court, the Sainsbury African Galleries house some of the ethnographical artefacts brought back from the Museum of Mankind. The space formerly occupied by the North Library now contains the Wellcome Gallery, funded by the Wellcome Trust

▲ Pages 56–57, left to right: two
  views of the Reading Room
  and the East Wing façade; the
  pedestrian bridge connecting
  the restaurant level to the
  galleries in the North Wing;
  and the café at the north-west
  corner of the court.
◄ The museum forecourt, on
  Great Russell Street, is a more
  attractive and dignified space
  now that it has been restored
  to its original design.

and opened in 2003, which, with flanking gallery spaces, is the focus for the Museum's ethnographical displays and the first gallery that most visitors encounter if entering the building from the north. It now seems extraordinary that so many treasures relating to African, Asian, Pacific and American cultures were exiled from the Museum for so long.

Indeed, it is already hard to imagine how the British Museum coped with its huge tide of visitors without the resource of the Great Court, now the first destination of most visitors to the building, a place of orientation and welcome. The Great Court allows visitors to identify those galleries and collections that they wish to see, to find directions to them and introductory material about them and later, perhaps, to return to the heart of the Museum for refreshment before striking out into new areas of the building. The processional march through gallery after gallery is now a course taken only by those who wish to experience the collections in this way.

Having created a great public space on a strikingly grand scale, the Museum had no intention of filling it with a clutter of objects. Information desks provide a vital facility for visitors and a heavily used café, with

▶ The restaurant, housed
in the upper level,
nestles underneath
the extraordinary roof.

moveable furniture, operates from the northern side of the Great Court. Only a few large artefacts are shown here – they include the stone lion unearthed at Cnidus in 1856, Egyptian heads and the Hoa Hakananai'a statue from Easter Island.

Norman Foster's Great Court project has created much more than a great covered public space: it has transformed the visitor's perception of the British Museum and has underscored the quality and signifi-cance of Smirke's building as a great and pioneering work of Neoclassicism – preceding, for example, Schinkel's Altes Museum in Berlin. Fundamental to

Foster's vision was the idea of the new through route across the Great Court from north to south. As part of the project, the forecourt of the Museum on Great Russell Street, which had become a somewhat cluttered space, partly used for parking, was restored to the for-mal order conceived by Smirke, with stone enclosures surrounding areas of grass. Ramps providing easy access for wheelchair users were seamlessly integrat-ed. To the north, Montague Place, where the Edward VII building faces the monumental London University Sen-ate House of the 1930s, has been closed to through traffic and landscaped, providing a convenient drop off

point for coach parties visiting the Museum as well as an attractive point of entry for many other visitors.

For Norman Foster, the Great Court is a project with significant roots, for example in the visionary projects of the American architect R. Buckminster Fuller, a major influence on Foster's thinking, as well as the progressive glass and iron structures of the Victorian age. A key theme in Foster's architecture over four decades has been the controlled use of natural light to create inspirational and environmentally benign internal spaces. This is reflected in built projects as diverse as the Sainsbury Centre, the Berlin Reichstag, Chek Lap Kok airport in Hong Kong, and London's Canary Wharf Underground station and is fundamental to the Great Court. One of Foster's major contributions to the renewal and renaissance of London has been his thinking on public space and urban connections. The ambitious project launched in 1997 as World Squares for All has already seen Trafalgar Square transformed as an accessible public space extending from the walls of the National Gallery and Foster is now working on proposals to reconfigure Parliament Square as something more than the traffic island that it has been for half a century. Like his daringly engineered Millennium Bridge,

- ◀ Exterior view of the Great Court roof, looking to the south.
- ▶ The Reading Room illuminated during a reception for museum staff, 2000. The interior decoration scheme is now visible from the courtyard through the windows.

connecting St Paul's Cathedral and Tate Modern, the Great Court is one of a new series of pedestrian links across London. The British Museum, once an impenetrable obstruction on the route from Covent Garden into Bloomsbury and Euston, is now a convenient connection.

A former Director has described the British Museum, the world's first national public museum, as "an exciting place to work, an exciting place to visit ... the greatest museum in the world". The Great Court has reaffirmed the Museum's global status as an incomparable treasure house of great works of art and antiquity and allowed it to rethink its role in a new century.

This edition © Scala Publishers Ltd, 2005
Text © Kenneth Powell, 2005

First published in 2005 by
Scala Publishers Ltd
Northburgh House
10 Northburgh Street
London EC1V 0AT

ISBN 1 85759 380 4

Designed by Andrew Shoolbred
Edited by Oliver Craske
Printed in Spain
10 9 8 7 6 5 4 3 2 1

All images by Nigel Young except as follows:
© The Trustees of The British Museum: 10, 12, 15, 27, 34
Foster and Partners: 21, 22–23, 24, 25, 36
Getty Images: 6, 8, 9, 14, 16, 17
John Hewitt: 48

Every effort has been made to acknowledge copyright of images where applicable. Any errors or omissions are unintentional and should be brought to the attention of the publishers.

The publishers would like to thank Andrew Thatcher, Paul Gardner and Kathryn Tollervey for their kind assistance.

◀◀ Front Cover: The inside of the Great Court, viewed from the south-east corner.
▶▶ Back cover and pages 2–3: Exterior view of the illuminated Great Court, viewed from the north at night.
◀ Page 1: Detail of the roof, the Reading Room drum, and the east portico.